An a-maze-ing colorful adventure!

DRAGON MAZES

Roger Moreau

STERLING

New York / London
www.sterlingpublishing.com/kids

⊰DEDICATION⊱

This book is dedicated to my daughter Lisa,
who loves the magical world

STERLING and the distinctive Sterling logo are registered trademarks of
Sterling Publishing Co., Inc.

10 9 8 7 6 5 4 3 2

Published by Sterling Publishing Co., Inc.
387 Park Avenue South, New York, NY 10016
© 2008 by Roger Moreau
Distributed in Canada by Sterling Publishing
c/o Canadian Manda Group, 165 Dufferin Street
Toronto, Ontario, Canada M6K 3H6
Distributed in the United Kingdom by GMC Distribution Services
Castle Place, 166 High Street, Lewes, East Sussex, England BN7 1XU
Distributed in Australia by Capricorn Link (Australia) Pty. Ltd.
P.O. Box 704, Windsor, NSW 2756, Australia

Sterling ISBN-13: 978-1-4027-4735-9
ISBN-10: 1-4027-4735-7

For information about custom editions, special sales, premium and
corporate purchases, please contact Sterling Special Sales
Department at 800-805-5489 or specialsales@sterlingpublishing.com.

CONTENTS

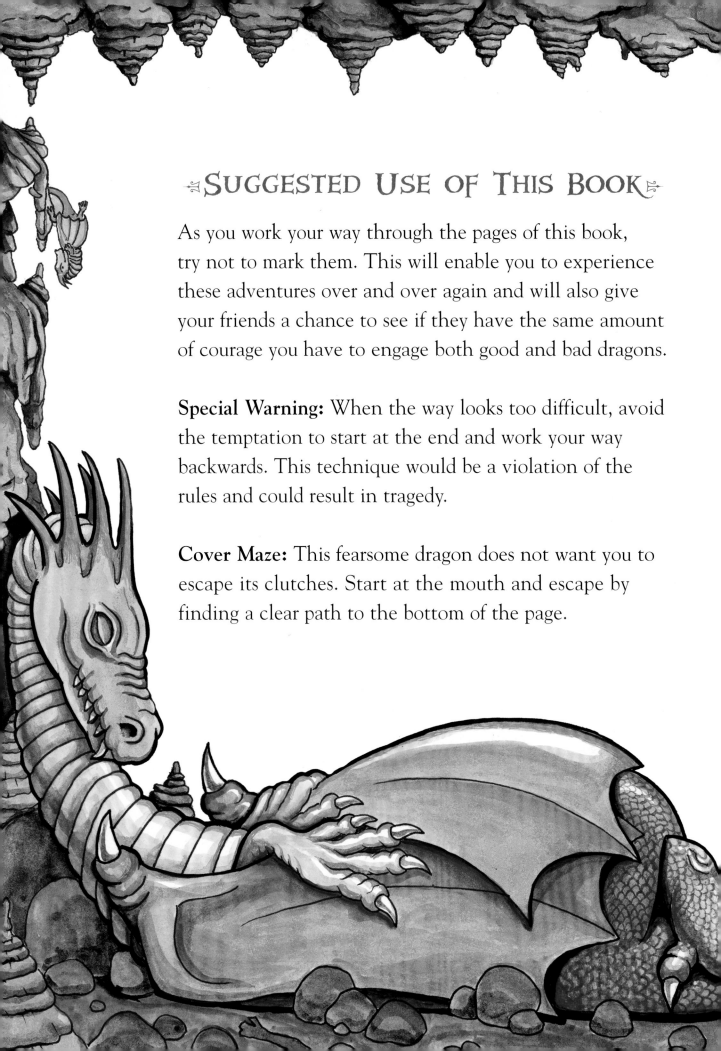

⊰SUGGESTED USE OF THIS BOOK⊱

As you work your way through the pages of this book, try not to mark them. This will enable you to experience these adventures over and over again and will also give your friends a chance to see if they have the same amount of courage you have to engage both good and bad dragons.

Special Warning: When the way looks too difficult, avoid the temptation to start at the end and work your way backwards. This technique would be a violation of the rules and could result in tragedy.

Cover Maze: This fearsome dragon does not want you to escape its clutches. Start at the mouth and escape by finding a clear path to the bottom of the page.

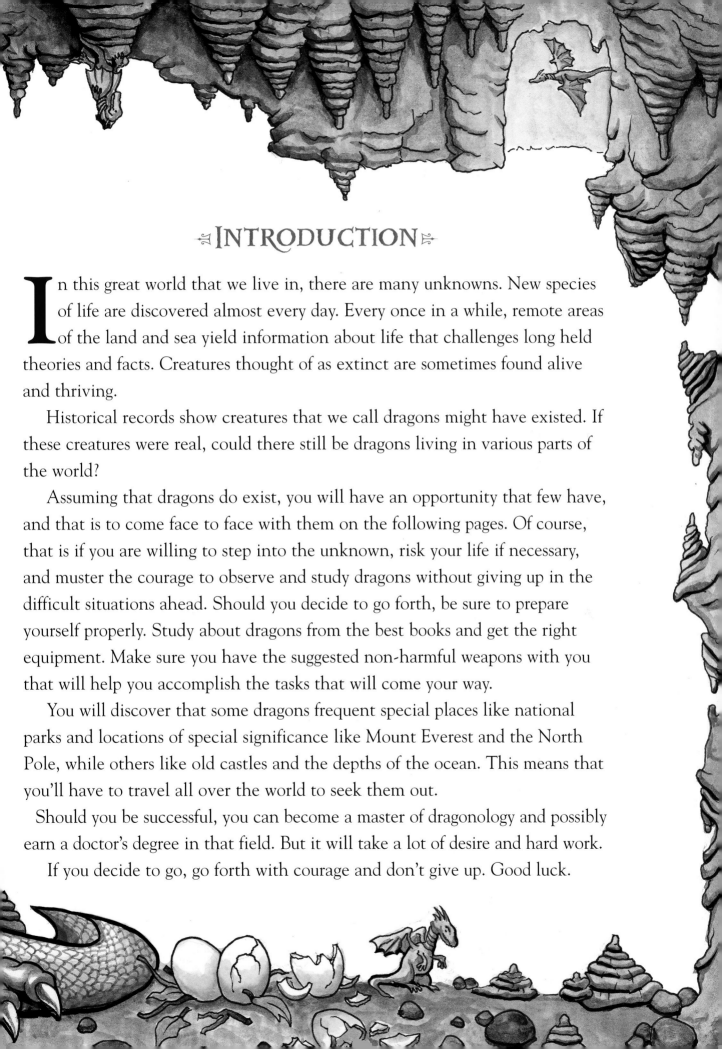

☙ INTRODUCTION ☙

In this great world that we live in, there are many unknowns. New species of life are discovered almost every day. Every once in a while, remote areas of the land and sea yield information about life that challenges long held theories and facts. Creatures thought of as extinct are sometimes found alive and thriving.

Historical records show creatures that we call dragons might have existed. If these creatures were real, could there still be dragons living in various parts of the world?

Assuming that dragons do exist, you will have an opportunity that few have, and that is to come face to face with them on the following pages. Of course, that is if you are willing to step into the unknown, risk your life if necessary, and muster the courage to observe and study dragons without giving up in the difficult situations ahead. Should you decide to go forth, be sure to prepare yourself properly. Study about dragons from the best books and get the right equipment. Make sure you have the suggested non-harmful weapons with you that will help you accomplish the tasks that will come your way.

You will discover that some dragons frequent special places like national parks and locations of special significance like Mount Everest and the North Pole, while others like old castles and the depths of the ocean. This means that you'll have to travel all over the world to seek them out.

Should you be successful, you can become a master of dragonology and possibly earn a doctor's degree in that field. But it will take a lot of desire and hard work.

If you decide to go, go forth with courage and don't give up. Good luck.

Dragon Facts and Equipment

Here are some valuable facts. There are good and bad dragons. Be very cautious when dealing with bad dragons. Bad dragons are very dangerous and destructive. Be especially careful of fire-breathing dragons. While good dragons can breathe fire, they will never use it in a destructive or harmful way. Good dragons can also be dangerous, however, but only if their lives and babies are threatened. Not all dragons breathe fire, which means that a bad dragon might not be a fire breather, so be cautious here and treat all dragons with great care and caution.

The following equipment will be useful to have:

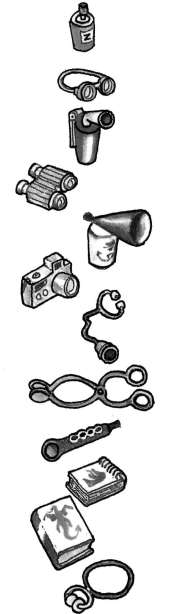

Sleeping Spray: To put dragons to sleep when they are close.

Fire Goggles: To protect your eyes from fire.

Fire Extinguisher: To put out fires.

Binoculars: To locate distant dragons.

Noise Blaster: To scare off dragons.

Digital Camera: To get photos of all dragons.

Stethoscope: To check out a dragon's heartbeat.

Tooth Extractor: To pull dragon teeth.

Flute: To put dragons to sleep from a distance.

Note Pad: To record your experience.

Dragonology Book: To learn about dragons.

Nose Clip: To protect against dragon breath.

LIBRARY

Find a path on the white tiles to the ladder. As you climb the ladder, total the numbers across each row and place the total on the book at the right. Read the book with the highest number.

THE EQUIPMENT ROOM

Find your way to each table to get your equipment and check out at the cash register.
Your path must be continuous without backtracking.

End

THE GRAND CANYON

This dragon is drinking too much water.
Find a clear path downstream and scare him away.

End

HIGH-ALTITUDE DRAGONS

Study the nest of these dragons that live at the foot of Mount Everest. Use your noise blaster to scare them away. Find a clear path to the nest.

End

Start

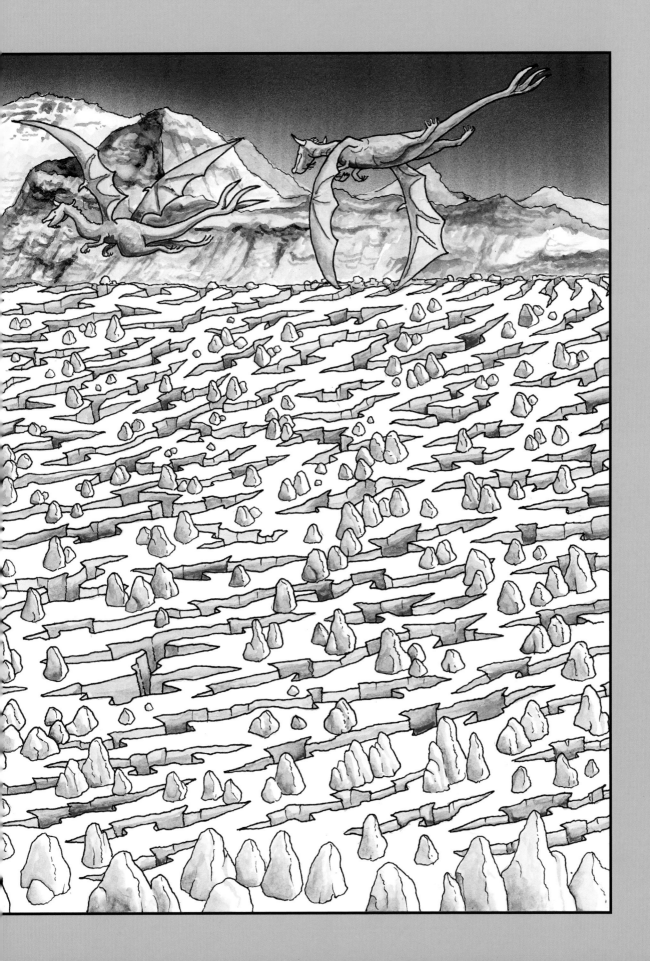

THE NORTH POLE

This dragon may look mean, but she's just building a nest for her babies.
Find a clear path to study her snow-breathing abilities.

Start

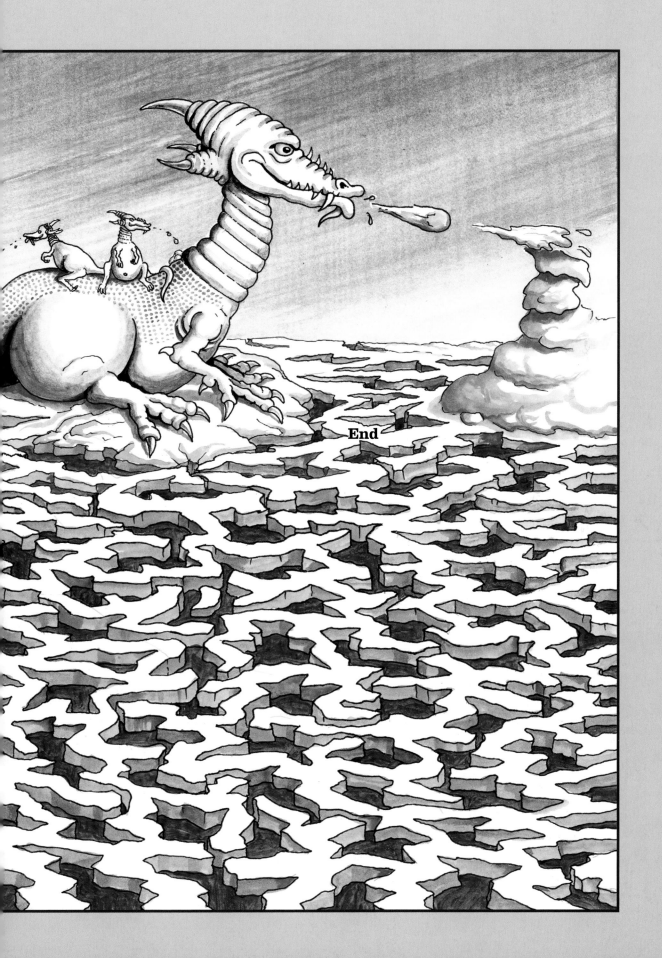

End

LAVA EATERS

These fire-breathing dragons eat lava. How can that be? Find a clear path to the eruption to find out. Be sure to wear protective goggles.

Start

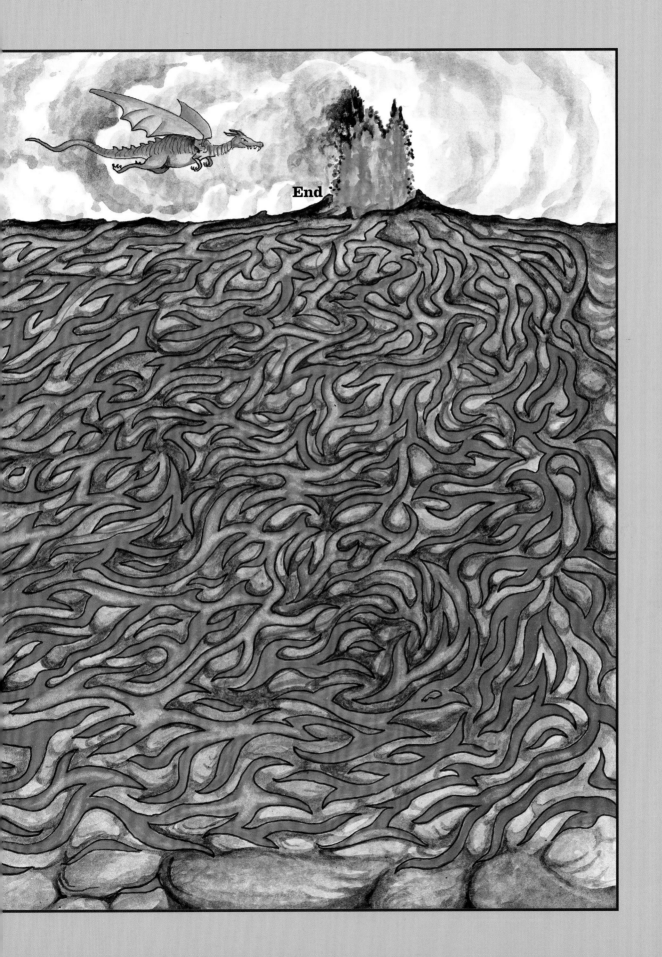

End

BRISTOL PINE CONE EATERS

These Bristol (England) pine cones are thousands of years old. They need protection.
Find a clear path and scare this dragon away with the noise blaster.

≈Angel Falls≈

There are two caves that are near Angel Falls. Only one is where these dragons live.
Which one? Find a clear path to the one that is their home.

Start

She's sound asleep. Find a clear path to her and check her heartbeat with the stethoscope. Don't wake her.

Start

End

THE THREE-HEADED FIRE BREATHER

All three heads of this dragon might be asleep. Let's hope so.
Find a clear path to the head at the right and extract a tooth for study.

Start

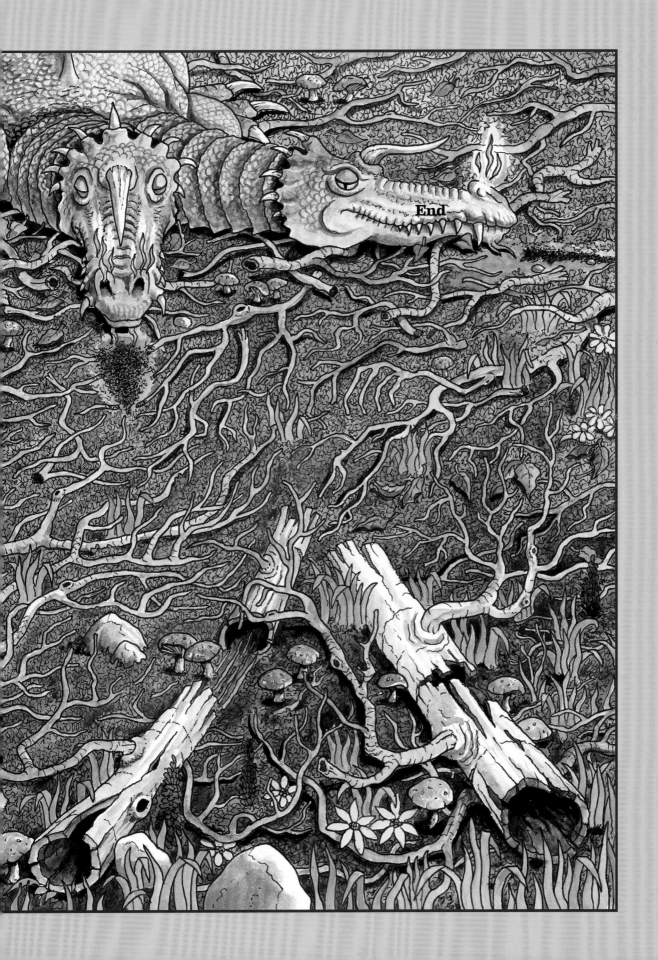

End

⇛ FIREBALLS ⇚

Study this dragon's ability to breathe fireballs by finding a clear path to its mouth.
Take your fire extinguisher.

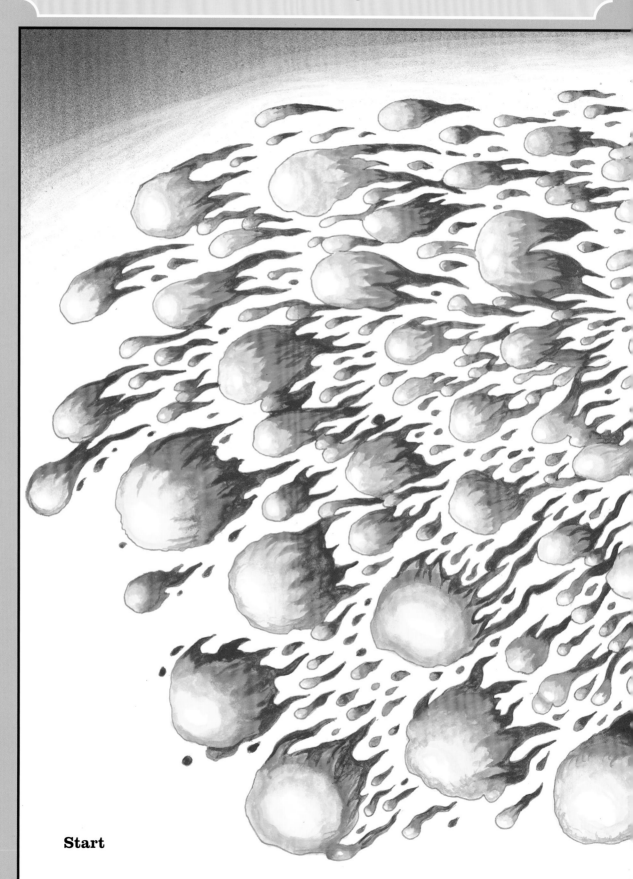

Start

End

THE EGG EATER

One of these dragons eats eggs. The mother of the eggs is not happy. Which one is the egg eater? The right path will take you to her. Use your flute to put them both to sleep.

Start

TERROR FROM THE SKIES

Quick, find a clear path to put out the fire and scare these dragons away.
Use the fire extinguisher to put out the flames.

Start

End

THE NUCLEAR POWER PLANT

If these fire breathers get some nuclear energy, they could become radioactive.
Shut off the power by turning the correct valve. But which valve?

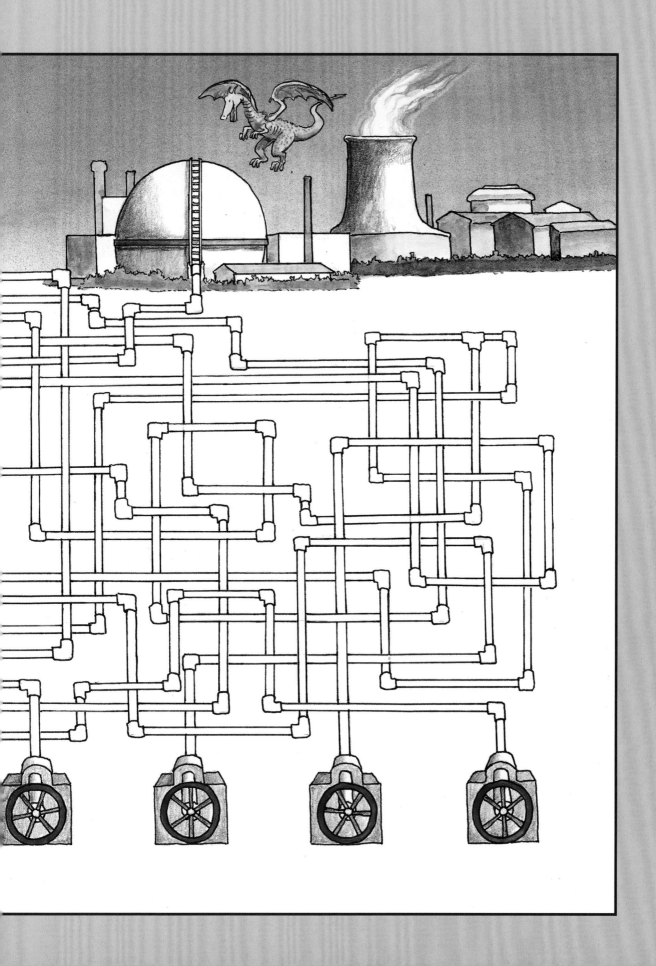

BAVARIAN CASTLE DRAGONS

Castle dragons could cause damage to these beautiful Bavarian castles.
Find your way to one of the castles to scare them off.

Start

End

THE TOWER

Find a path up the light-colored bricks to scare off that shingle-eating dragon.

Continue up to the shingle roof and along the light-colored shingles to
scare off the dragon. Use the noise blaster.

End

Start

THE TREASURE ROOM

This is a treasure-loving dragon that is not going to give up his treasure.
Find a clear path and put him to sleep with a good blast of sleeping spray.

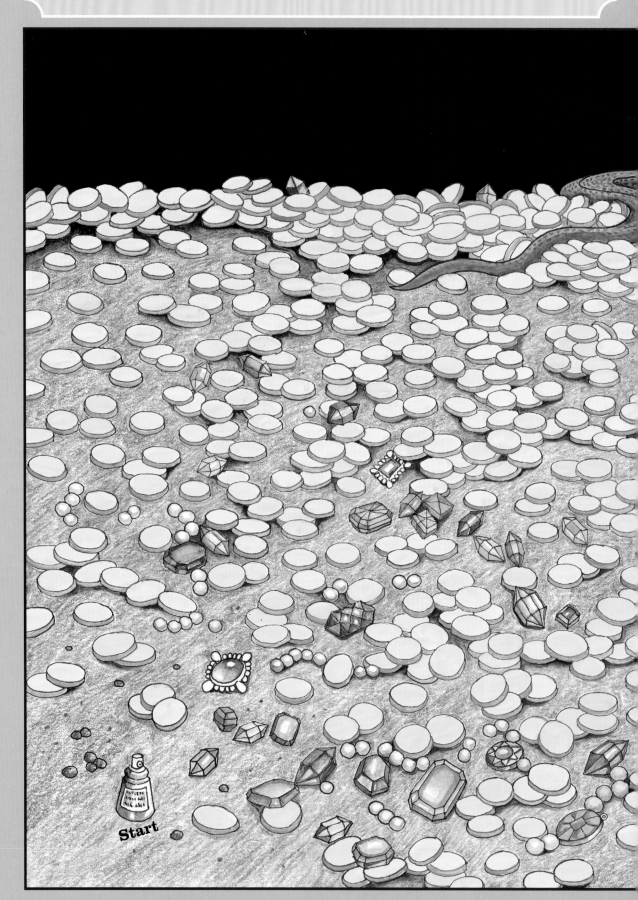

Start

End

MAIDEN IN DISTRESS

This poor maiden is frightened stiff. You'll have to free her by finding two paths to each dragon head. Put each head to sleep with the sleeping spray and help the maiden to freedom.

Start

End

THE SEA DRAGON

While this mother is off finding food, find a clear path to study the babies below.

Start

End

THE SEA DRAGON CONTINUED

Continue down to the bottom where the babies live.

MOTHER'S DISTRESS

Fishermen have hooked into the sea dragon's baby. You must find
a clear path to unhook the baby and hopefully save the fishermen.

Start

End

⊰SAVE THE BABY⊱

This dragon's baby has fallen from its nest. It is still alive.
Haul it up the cliff by climbing a continuous crack to the nest.

End

Start

44

⚜SAVE THE BABY CONTINUED⚜

Continue to the nest. Mother will thank you.

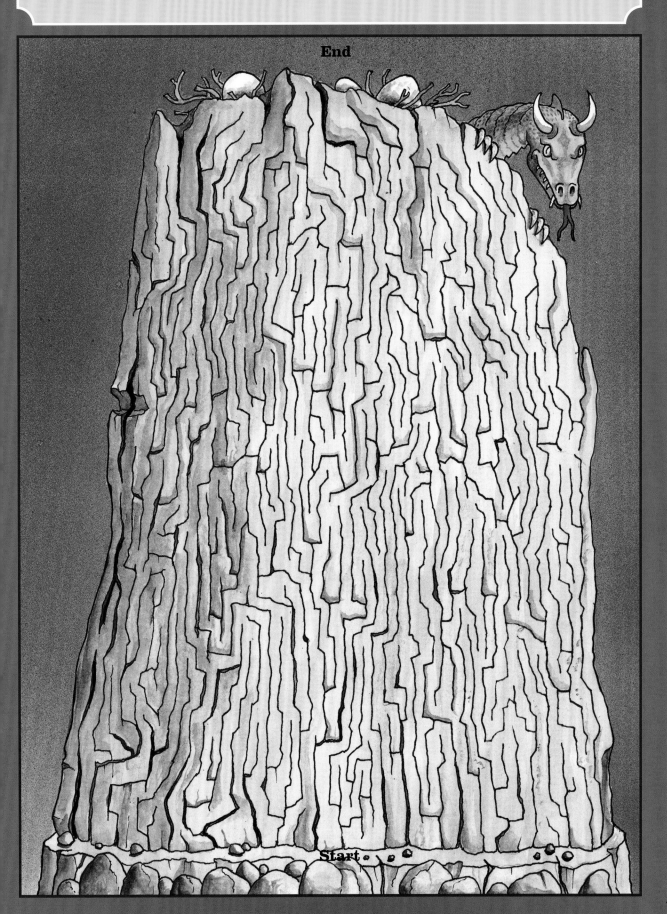

❧ TRAPPED ❧

This poor dragon has been caught in a hunter's trap. Free him by
finding a clear path and opening the trap.

Start

End

THE TOURNAMENT OF DRAGONS

The yearly tournament of the good against the bad dragons is about to begin.
Find a clear path to the stadium.

Start

End

LET THE BATTLE BEGIN

The good dragons are on the left, and the bad on the right. Start on the left and select any dragon to blast on the right. Follow the fire blast along one patch to see if it's a hit that will take out the dragon. The next shot must be from the right to the left. Continue alternating until one side is eliminated. Who will win?

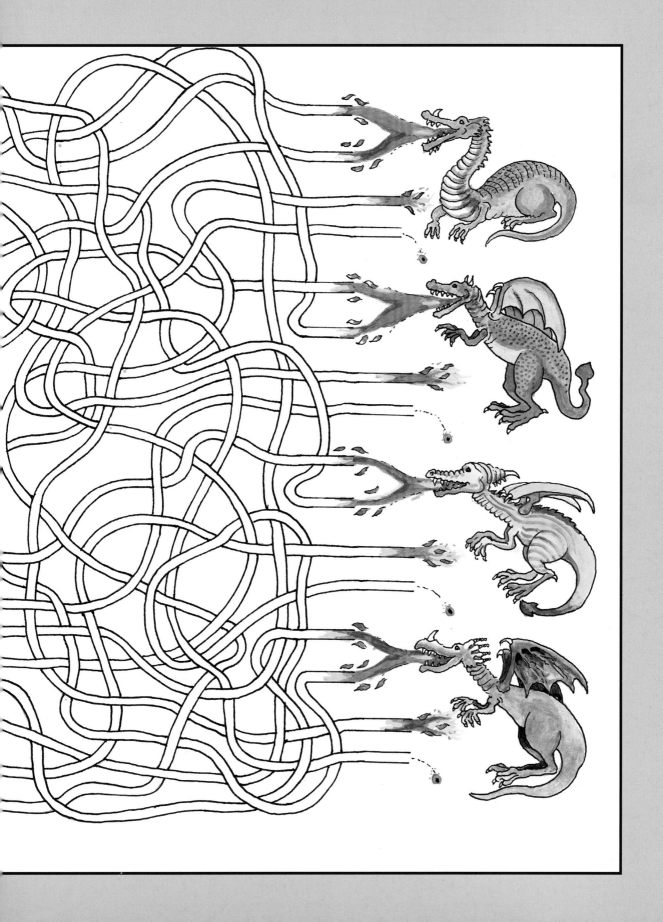

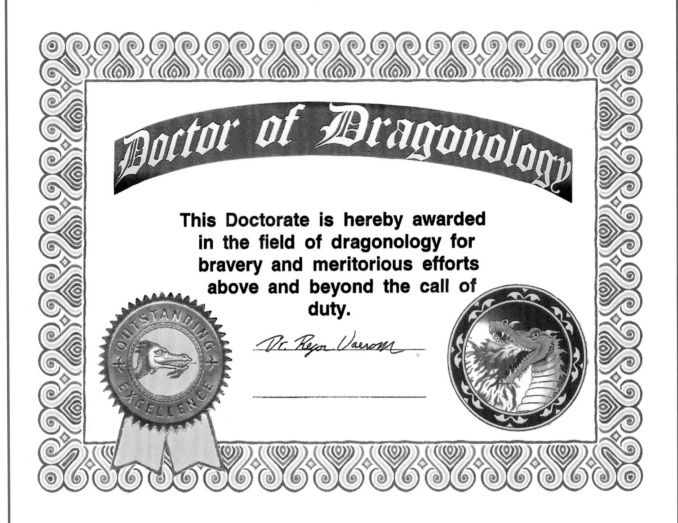

☙ CONGRATULATIONS ☙

You have performed to the highest abilities that can be expected of anyone. You have been successful at studying many different species of dragons (helping dragonologists to understand them better), faced dangerous situations in a quest to help mankind, and performed kind tasks for peace-loving dragons. The department of Dragonology is therefore proud to honor you with this diploma of Doctor of Dragonology. Put your name on the blank space on the certificate above. It is hoped that you continue your work in this field. Your perseverance, courage, and determination are assets that will undoubtedly assist you throughout your life.

If you have any trouble along the way—and I'm sure you didn't—refer to the following pages. They are the solutions to the mazes.

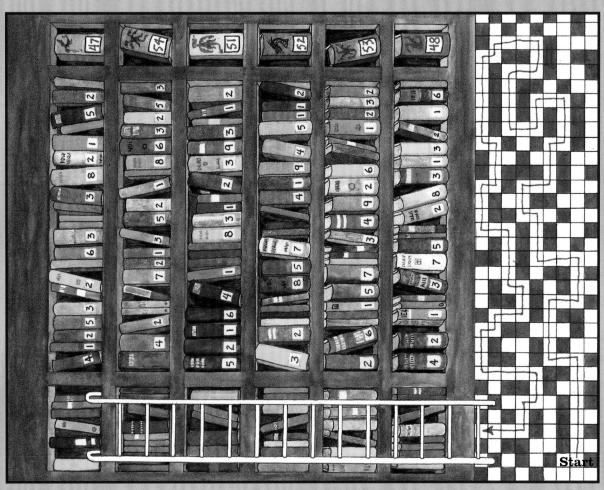

Cover Maze/Library

Start

53

The Equipment Room

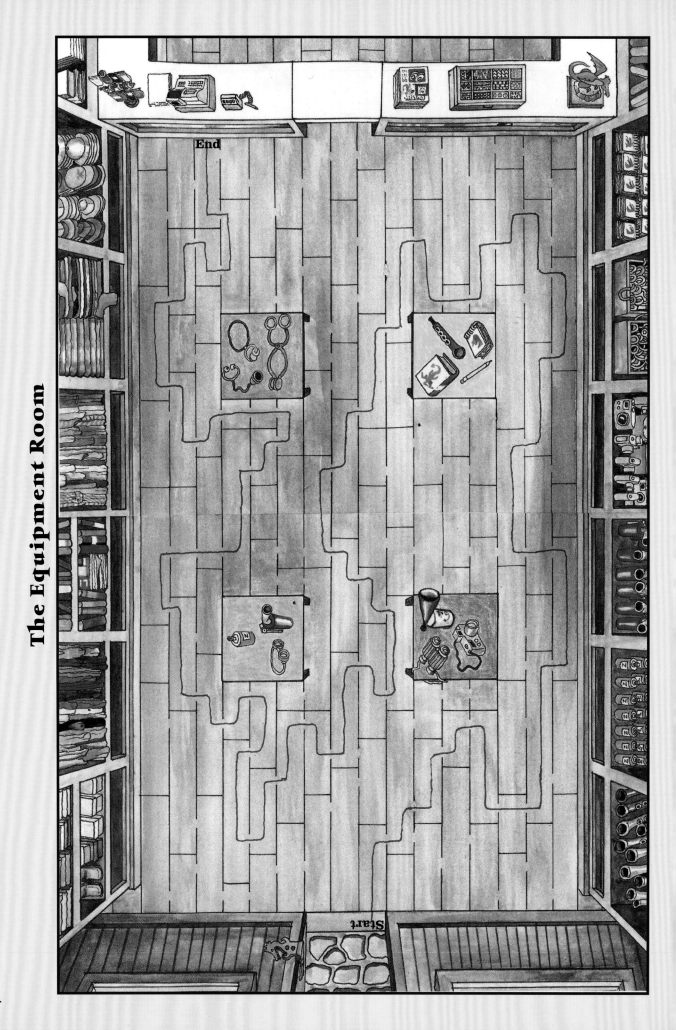

The Grand Canyon

Start

Exit

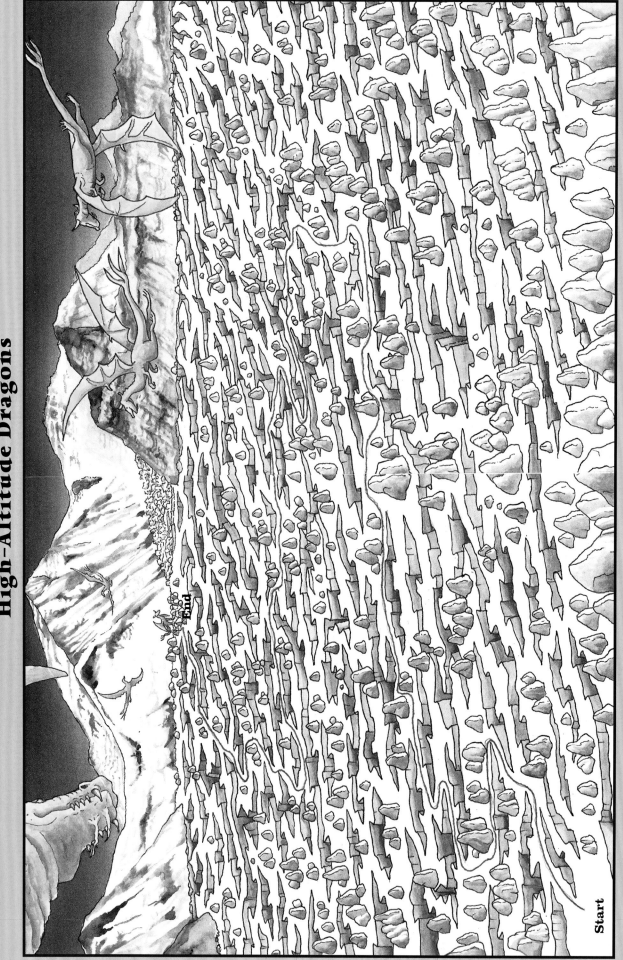

Start

End

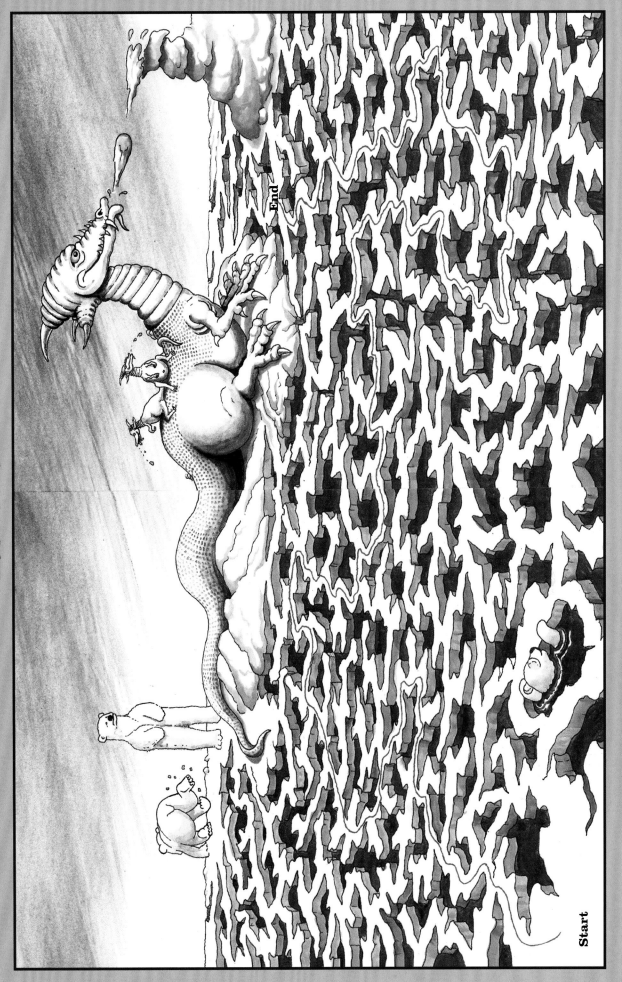

Lava Eaters

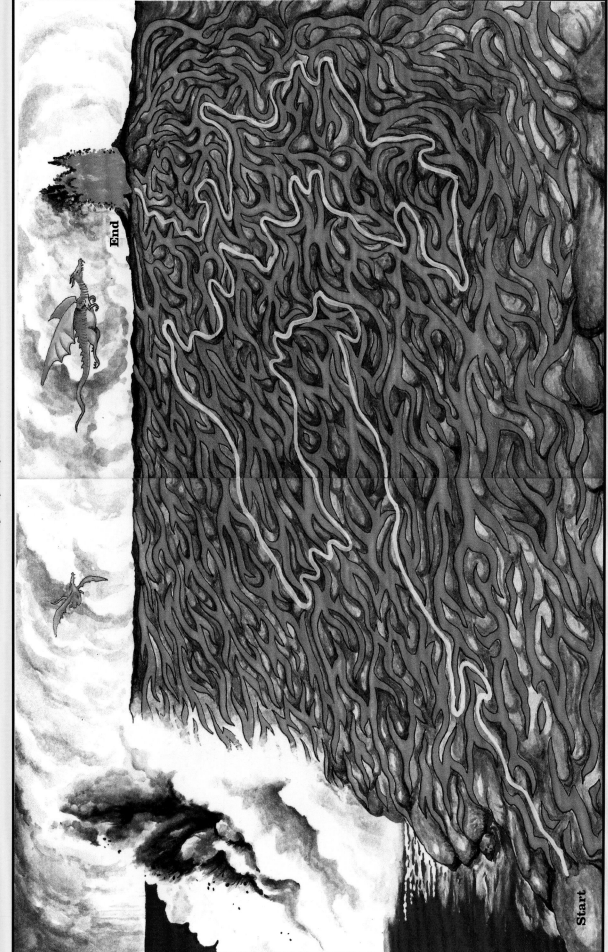

Start

End

Bristol Pine Cone Eaters

Angel Falls

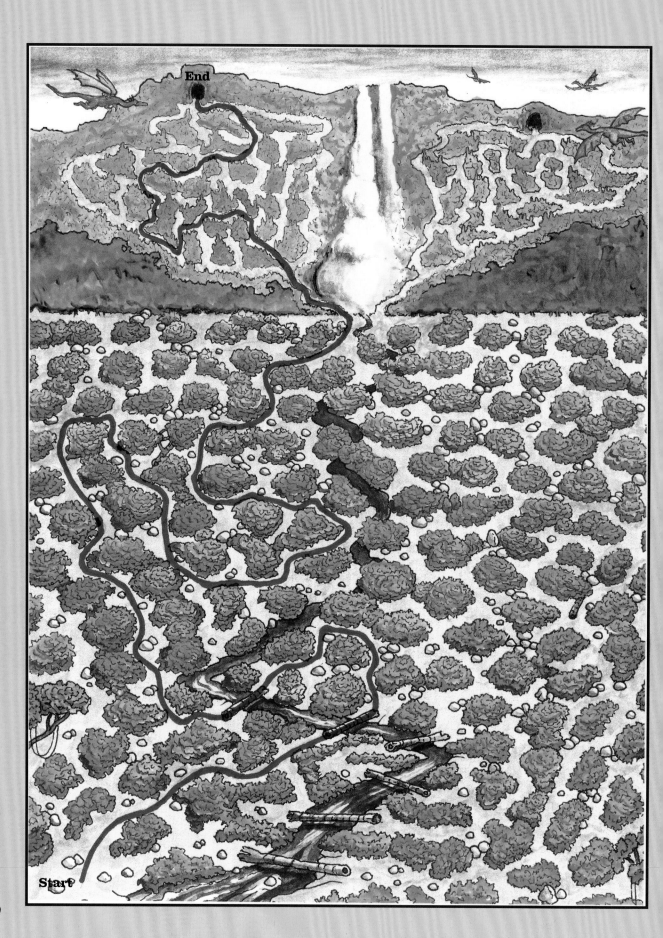

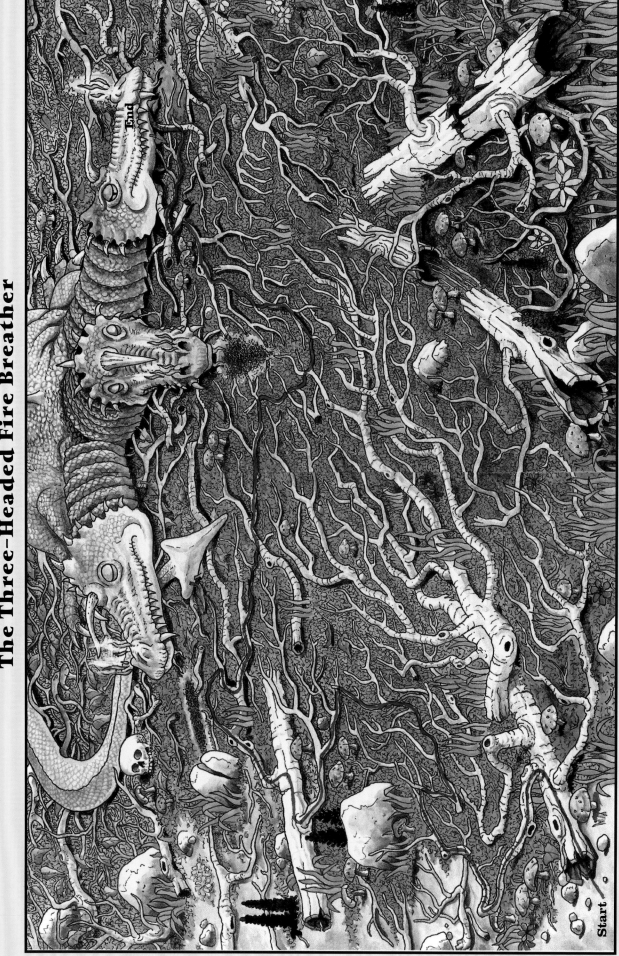

The Three-Headed Fire Breather

62

Fireballs

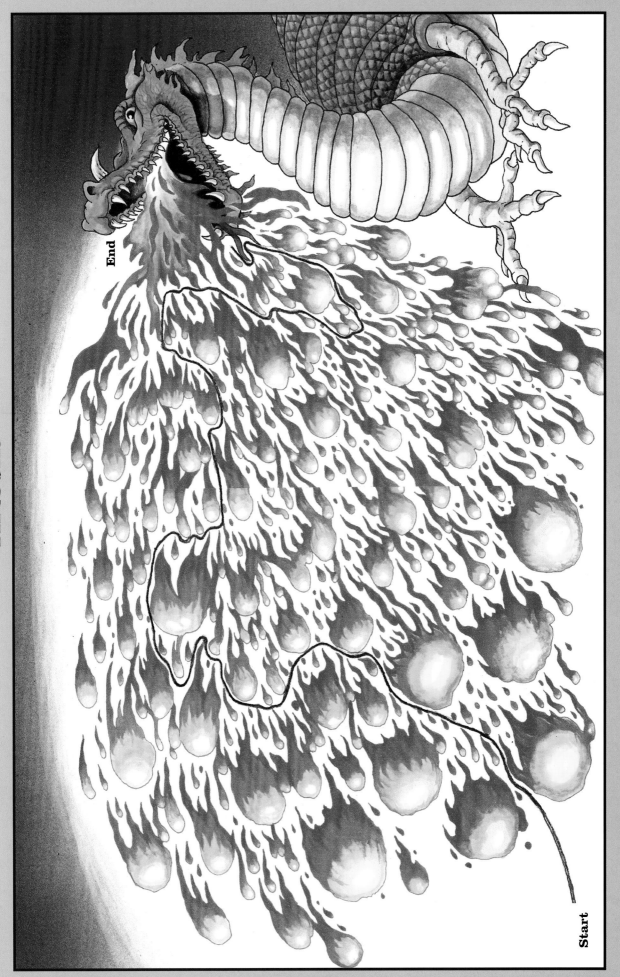

End

Start

The Egg Eater

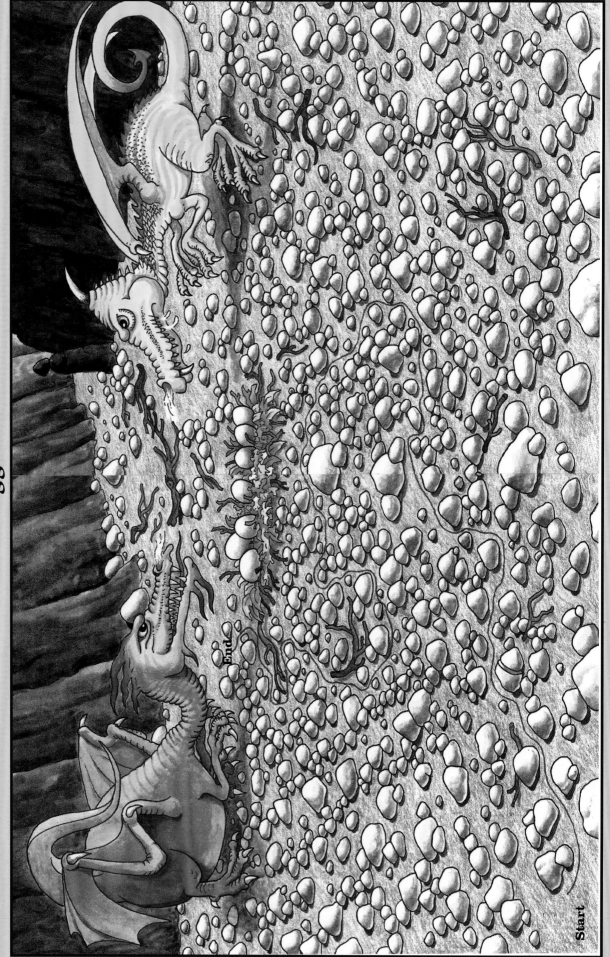

Start

End

Terror From the Skies

End

Start

The Nuclear Power Plant

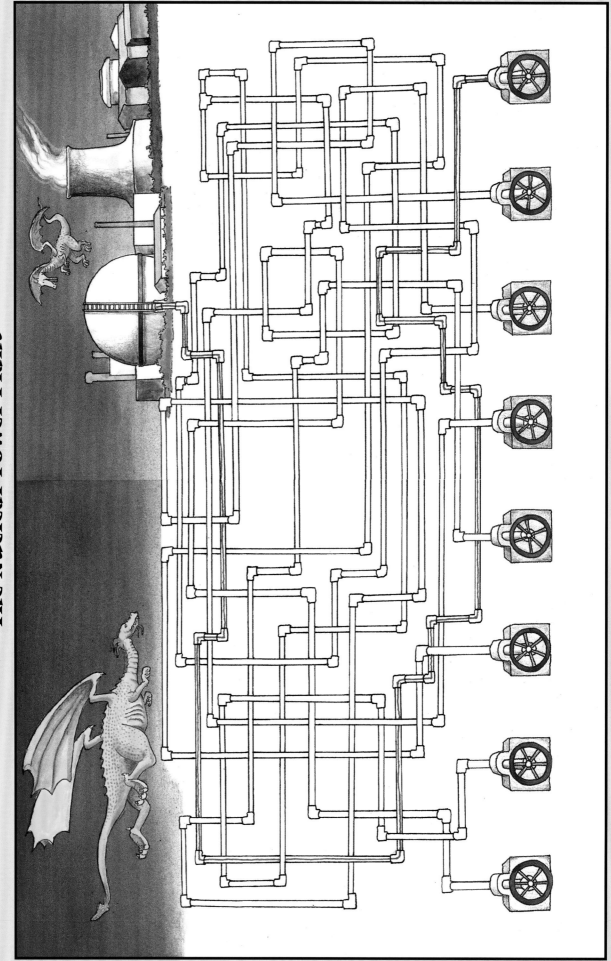

Bavarian Castle Dragons

Start

End

The Tower

Start

End

The Tower Continued

End

Start

The Treasure Room

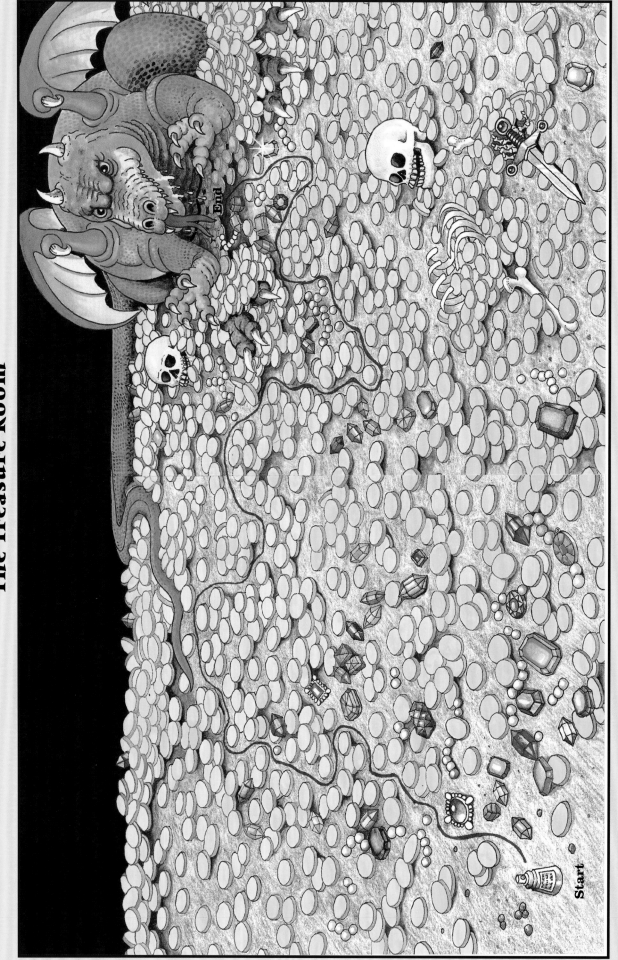

Start

End

Maiden in Distress

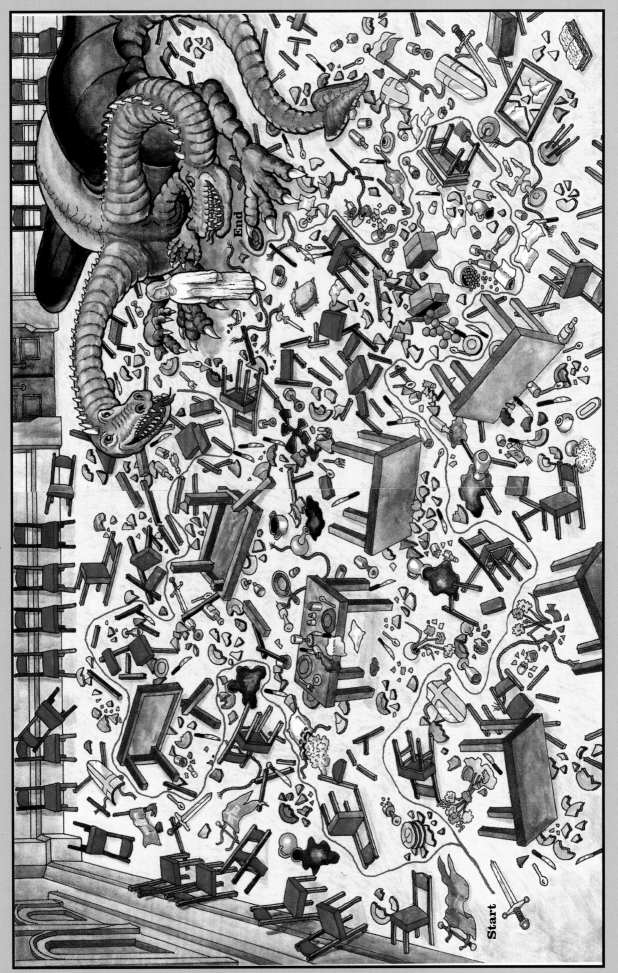

Start

End

The Sea Dragon

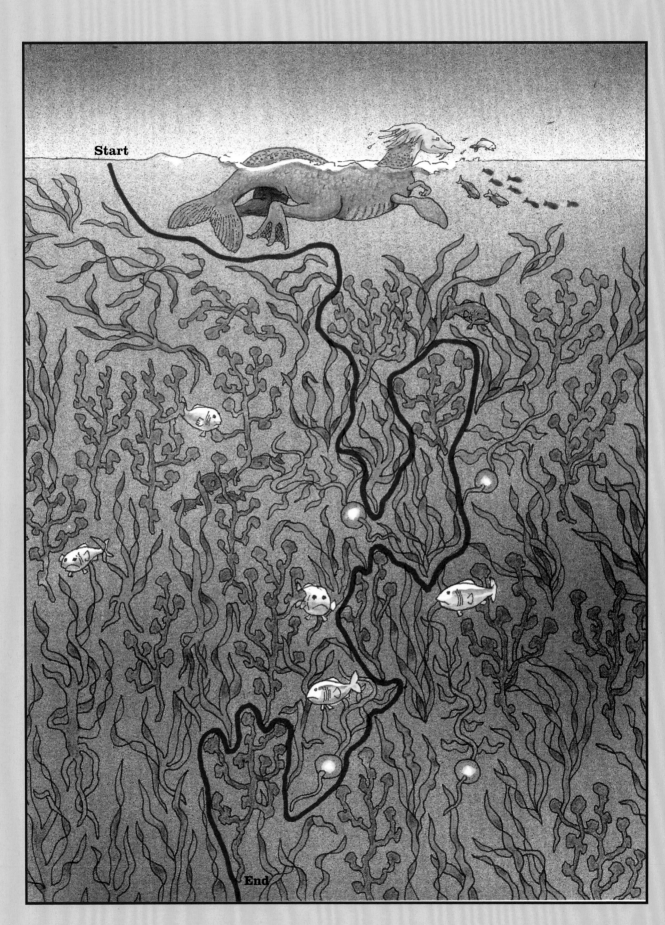

Start

End

The Sea Dragon Continued

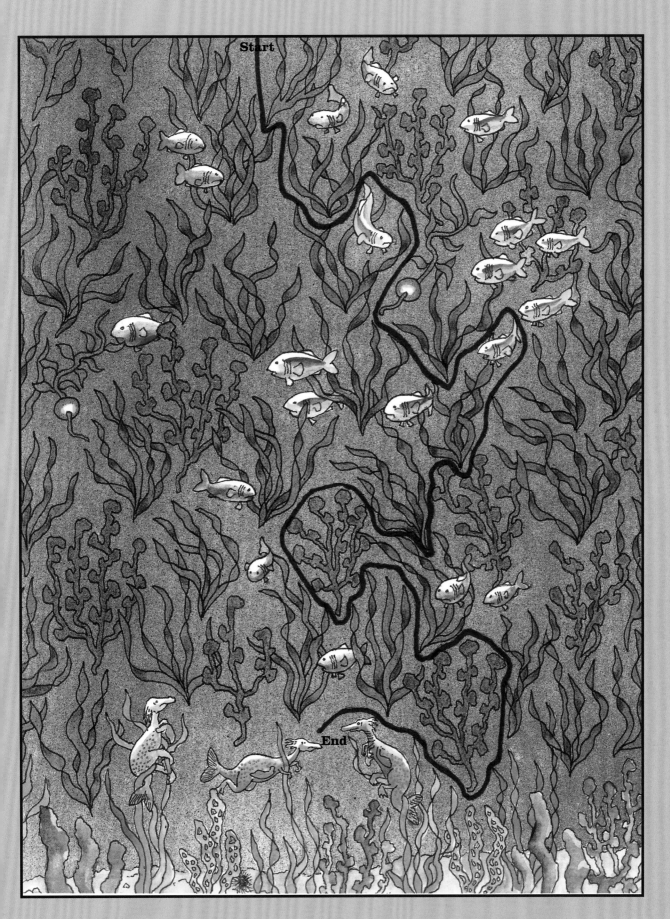

Save the Baby

Start

End

Save the Baby Continued

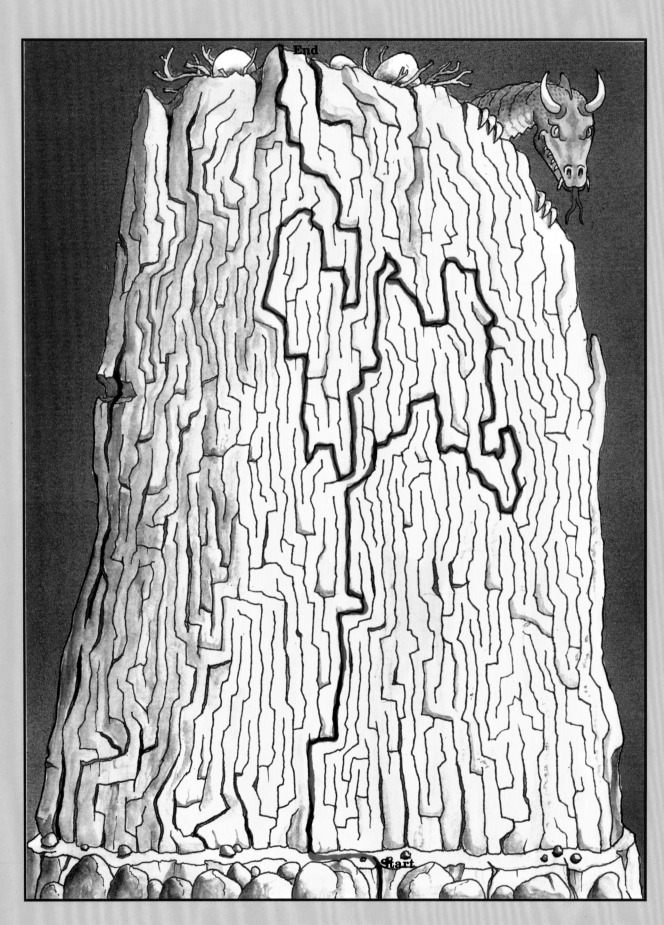

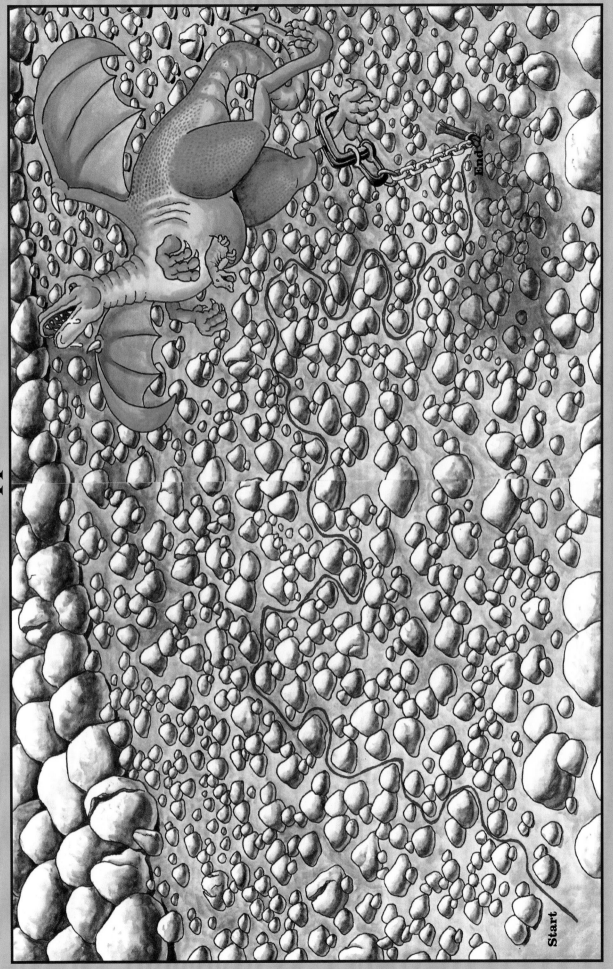

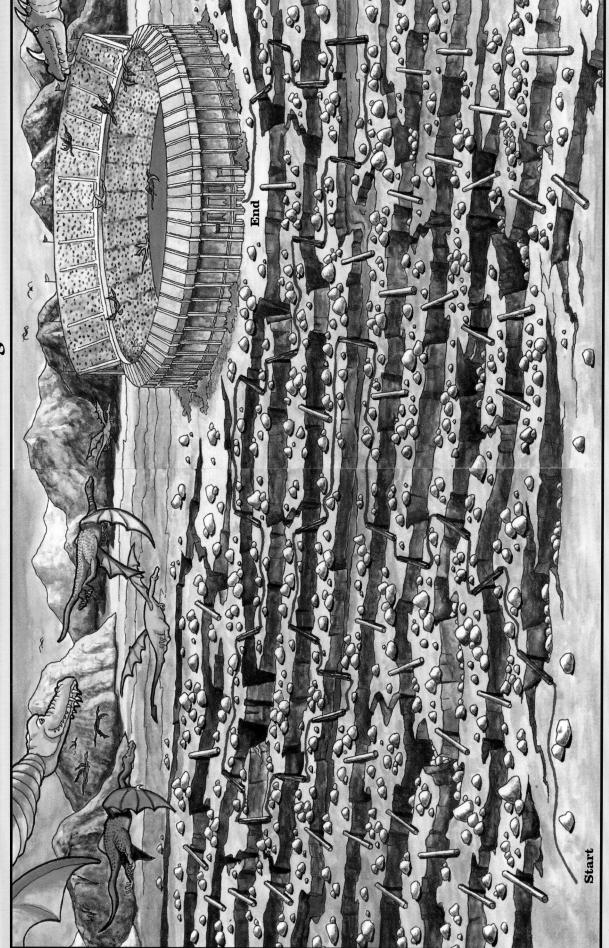

The Tournament of Dragons

Start

End

Let the Battle Begin

⊰ INDEX ⊱

Pages in **bold** refer to answer mazes.